# REVERSE YOUR  BAD KARMA

## The Good Thing to Do for the Bad Thing You Did

**ELLE DORIGHT**

**Avon, Massachusetts**

Copyright © 2012 by F+W Media, Inc.
All rights reserved.
This book, or parts thereof, may not be reproduced in any
form without permission from the publisher; exceptions are
made for brief excerpts used in published reviews.

Published by
Adams Media, a division of F+W Media, Inc.
57 Littlefield Street, Avon, MA 02322. U.S.A.
*www.adamsmedia.com*

ISBN 10: 1-4405-5243-6
ISBN 13: 978-1-4405-5243-4
eISBN 10: 1-4405-5244-4
eISBN 13: 978-1-4405-5244-1

Printed in the United States of America.

10 9 8 7 6 5 4 3 2 1

Contains material adapted and abridged from *1001 Ways to Do Good* by Meera Lester, copyright © 2008 by F+W Media, Inc., ISBN 10: 1-59869-474-X, ISBN 13: 978-1-59869-474-1.

This publication is designed to provide accurate and authoritative information with regard to the subject matter covered. It is sold with the understanding that the publisher is not engaged in rendering legal, accounting, or other professional advice. If legal advice or other expert assistance is required, the services of a competent professional person should be sought.
—From a *Declaration of Principles* jointly adopted by a Committee of the American Bar Association and a Committee of Publishers and Associations

Certain sections of this book deal with activities that would be in violation of various federal, state, and local laws if actually carried out. We do not advocate the breaking of any law. The authors, Adams Media, and F+W Media, Inc., do not accept liability for any injury, loss, legal consequence, or incidental or consequential damage incurred by reliance on the information or advice provided in this book. The information in this book is for entertainment purposes only.

Many of the designations used by manufacturers and sellers to distinguish their product are claimed as trademarks. Where those designations appear in this book and Adams Media was aware of a trademark claim, the designations have been printed with initial capital letters.

*This book is available at quantity discounts for bulk purchases.*
*For information, please call 1-800-289-0963.*

# CONTENTS

**Introduction:** How to Use This Book
4

**Reverse Your Bad Karma** for Humanity
5

**Reverse Your Bad Karma** for Nature
131

**Reverse Your Bad Karma** for Order
187

**Reverse Your Book!**
287

# Introduction:
# How to Use This Book

You're not perfect. Nobody is. We've all done things we're not proud of. Maybe you gossiped. Maybe you lied. Maybe you held up a liquor store. That's okay.

*Reverse Your Bad Karma* isn't here to judge you. We're here to help you figure out what to do next. Whether you served a vegetarian mock chicken that was actually real, or fed your puppy dog food that was actually made of dog. It doesn't matter. The important thing is that you're sorry.

You are sorry, right?

Of course you are. Remember, what goes around comes around. And if you killed the last Bengal Tiger, something very, very bad could be coming your way. You don't want to be an earthworm in your next life.

That's where *Reverse Your Bad Karma* comes in. Use this book, and you'll have a clear conscience in no time!

On each left-hand page you'll find a bad thing you did, whether you cheated on a test or executed the perfect Ponzi scheme. On the opposite page, you'll see what you have to do to *Reverse Your Bad Karma* and cancel out your devious deed.

Find the bad thing on the left, and then do the good thing on the right. And just like that, you've injected a little good karma into your life, and gotten back to a clean slate.

*Reverse Your Bad Karma:* Redemption's never been this easy!

# REVERSE YOUR BAD KARMA FOR HUMANITY

# "I am so wasted!"

—Jane Doe

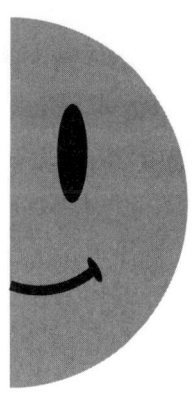

# "No act of kindness, no matter how small, is ever wasted."

—Aesop

*What you did . . .*
## You stole Girl Scout cookies.

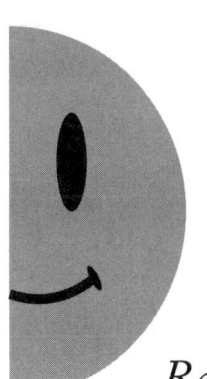

## *Reverse Your Bad Karma!*

*Become a volunteer crossing guard.* Some communities rely on volunteers to help kids get home safely. If your schedule allows, look into volunteering in the morning or afternoon for this important position.

*What you did . . .*

**You told your nephews that their daddy is Santa Claus— a drunk Santa Claus.**

## *Reverse Your Bad Karma!*

*Give gifts to a needy family at Christmas.* Rather than exchanging gifts between family members, organize a gift drive to be donated to a needy family outside the United States. You can either collect the actual gifts, or ask family members to donate the amount of money they would have spent on purchasing family gifts.

*What you did . . .*

**You crashed a random wedding ceremony and objected to the marriage.**

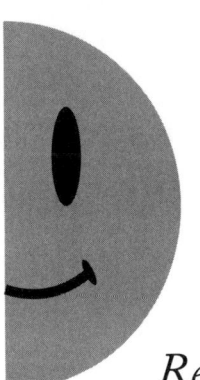

## *Reverse Your Bad Karma!*

*Keep a secret.* The next time a friend, relative, child, or business associate tells you something in confidence, do your utmost to honor them by keeping their secret.

*What you did...*

**You convinced a friend's child that their house was haunted. And that the ghost would get them unless they woke their parents up at 3 A.M. every night.**

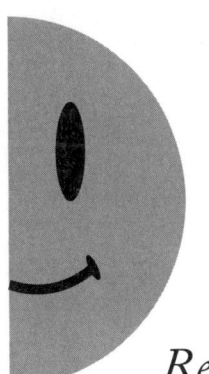

## *Reverse Your Bad Karma!*

*Help fix up a friend's home before she sells it.* You might pack boxes, wrap pictures and paintings in brown paper for shipping, put outdated documents through a shredder so they don't have to be part of the move, clean out the garage so excess furniture can be put there when the new carpet goes in, or go through the house with spackle and a trowel to patch small nail holes in preparation for the painters. A move is a huge transition for most of us. The help of friends is invaluable during that time.

*What you did . . .*

**You bought a lifetime supply of junk food and tried to pass it off as a corporate expense. (It was for a . . . client lunch? Maybe the client was a class of nine-year-olds?)**

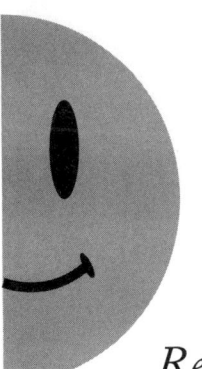

## *Reverse Your Bad Karma!*

*Pay for the person behind you.* Next time you pull up to the drive-thru window, pay for what you ordered and what the person behind you ordered. When it's his turn to pay, he'll be pleasantly surprised by your kind act.

*What you did* . . .

**You found a Canadian coin in your purse, and you gave it to a homeless man.**

## *Reverse Your Bad Karma!*

*Give money to a friend.* Drop an extra $20 bill into an envelope and send it anonymously to a friend of a friend who is a single mom or dad struggling to make ends meet.

*What you did . . .*

**You borrowed your roommate's favorite shirt . . .
for a paintball game.**

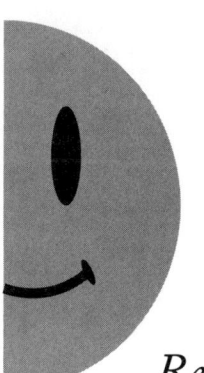

## *Reverse Your Bad Karma!*

*Patronize an eco-friendly dry cleaner.* These dry cleaners don't use chemicals that are harmful to the environment, and some even use recyclable cardboard hangers.

*What you did...*

**You cheated on your spouse. At your child's birthday party. With the magician.**

## *Reverse Your Bad Karma!*

*Smile often.* When others see you smile at them, they may feel suddenly lighter and less weighted by the pressures of the world. Your smile can lift the spirits of someone who is suffering or feeling dejected.

*What you did...*
**You stole candy from a baby.**

## *Reverse Your Bad Karma!*

*Do laundry for a new mom.* If a friend has recently had a baby, offer to wash, dry, and fold her clothes. She could use the time to nap when the baby is sleeping, and may still be less than 100 percent after giving birth.

*What you did...*

**You purposely drove your car through a puddle to spray dirty water on a pedestrian.**

## *Reverse Your Bad Karma!*

*Help someone change a flat tire, even if it's raining.* If you've ever had to change a flat tire on your own before, you know how much of a hassle it can be. So the next time you see someone changing a tire on the side of the road, pull over and offer an extra hand—even if it's just to hold an umbrella over his head.

*What you did . . .*
## You taught a kid to curse.

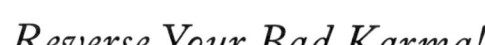

## *Reverse Your Bad Karma!*

*Let the neighborhood kids play in your yard.* Give them a nice, safe place to spend time while their parents are out.

*What you did...*

**You raced a pregnant woman for a seat on the bus, and you won.
(Yesss! In your face, waddler!)**

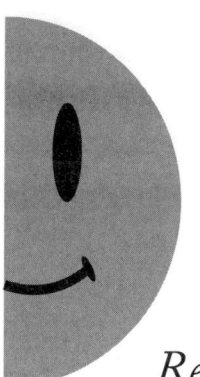

## *Reverse Your Bad Karma!*

*Let someone have the taxi you've just hailed.* Next time you hail a cab while it's busy on the street, let the person standing next to you have it. This simple gesture may cost a few minutes of your time, but it will mean the world to the stranger you helped.

*What you did* . . .

**You always let your dog off the leash when the mail carrier comes by.**

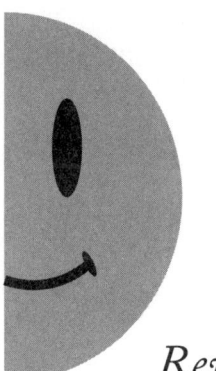

## *Reverse Your Bad Karma!*

*Prepare a hot drink for your mail carrier in winter.* Ready a cup of cocoa, tea, or coffee and have it waiting for the letter carrier out delivering mail on a cold and snowy day.

*What you did . . .*
## You started a cult.

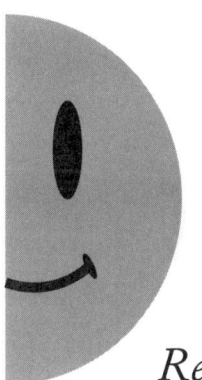

## Reverse Your Bad Karma!

*Inspire others.* Hang a picture of an inspirational individual in your home or office, and let him or her be an inspiration to you and others. Make a hero's wall going up the staircase wall to the landing. Put pictures of great social scientists, anthropologists, archaeologists, world leaders, women of achievement, accomplished athletes, skilled artisans, and others whose images will inspire others.

*What you did . . .*

**You bought the cheapest item on the newlywed's registry, and then switched cards at the reception with the biggest box on the gift table.**

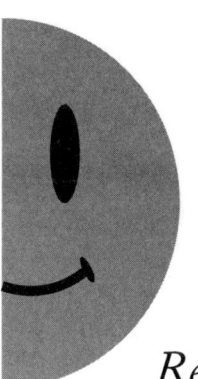

## *Reverse Your Bad Karma!*

*Collect new toys for homeless shelters.* Call on friends and family to donate toys after first calling a local shelter to find out its needs. Collect, wrap, and donate the toys for the holidays to the shelter's children.

*What you did* . . .

**You ordered 100 extra-large pepperoni pizzas . . . to be delivered to a Weight Watchers meeting.**

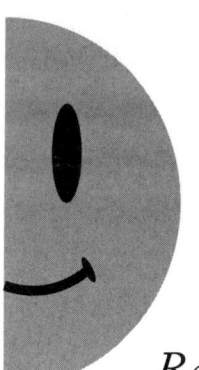

## *Reverse Your Bad Karma!*

*Organize a neighborhood food drive.* Get your neighbors to donate canned and nonperishable goods and give everything collected to a local food bank. Why not make this an event that is not tied to a holiday? Hungry people need food at all times of the year.

*What you did . . .*

# You spit your gum out onto a wheelchair ramp.

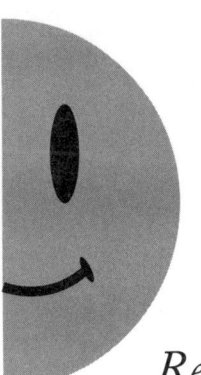

## *Reverse Your Bad Karma!*

*Pick up trash and sweep a dirty sidewalk.* It doesn't have to be your trash or your sidewalk.

*What you did . . .*

**You stole dinner off of an unattended grill in a stranger's backyard.**

## *Reverse Your Bad Karma!*

*Cook a meal for a relative with a new baby.* After the birth of a baby, everyone's so busy there's hardly any time to eat. Help out the family by putting together a homemade dinner and delivering it to their home.

*What you did ...*

**You regularly visit a children's hospital ... so that you can nab the toilet paper, light bulbs, and spare linens from the supply closets.**

## *Reverse Your Bad Karma!*

*Change out your regular light bulbs for compact fluorescents.* They screw in the socket the same way, but the fluorescent bulb uses only about 25 percent of the energy of an incandescent bulb. In addition, use of a compact fluorescent will keep about half a ton of carbon dioxide out of the atmosphere (over the life of the bulb).

*What you did...*

**Your friend told you a secret and begged you not to tell anyone. You didn't... you just tweeted it.**

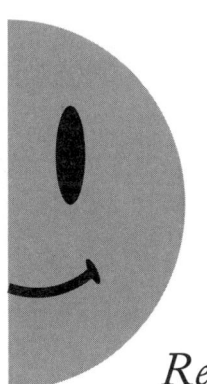

## *Reverse Your Bad Karma!*

*Do chores for a friend in a time of need.* You could make a meal, change bedding so she could have a good night's sleep, get her groceries, or run small errands to comfort your friend as she goes through her crisis.

*What you did . . .*

**You anonymously reported a fake health code violation for a restaurant because they took twenty minutes to bring you a glass of water (without ice, even!).**

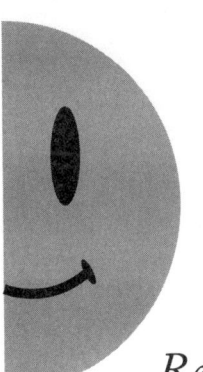

## *Reverse Your Bad Karma!*

*Let someone cut in front of you at the fast food counter.* You're giving the other person a head start to appease his thirst and hunger. It's a thoughtful thing to do, and it teaches your own body that you are in the driver's seat, not its slave.

*What you did . . .*

**You hid your grandpa's dentures.**

## *Reverse Your Bad Karma!*

*Help an elderly neighbor clean her yard.* Rake up any leaves, trim her hedges, and mow her lawn. Remove fallen dead tree limbs and brush from her yard. Tree limbs and brush can become a fire hazard.

*What you did . . .*

**You forgot to buy your son a bike helmet, so you wrapped his head in bubble wrap before he rode to school.**

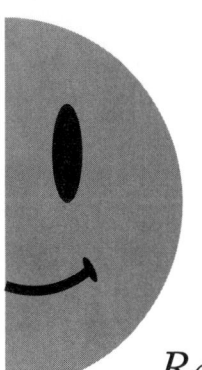

## *Reverse Your Bad Karma!*

*Prevent childhood obesity.* The growing American weight problem isn't just an adult issue. Make sure your child gets a balanced diet with plenty of fruits and vegetables. Ensure that snacks are healthy and that your child gets enough exercise each day.

*What you did . . .*

**You broke up a couple's engagement so that you could nab their wedding date at an exclusive garden conservatory.**

## *Reverse Your Bad Karma!*

*Make a donation to your local parks department.* Parks are for all to share—your contribution will help them become better places for everyone in your community to enjoy.

*What you did . . .*

**You sold an old mattress, even though you're pretty sure it had bedbugs.**

## *Reverse Your Bad Karma!*

*Share the housework with your mate.* Shouldering the workload together helps to keep your relationship healthier and less antagonistic than when one partner carries the entire burden. Split up the chores and they will be done in half the time.

*What you did . . .*

**You paid a bunch of kids to egg your boss's house.**

## *Reverse Your Bad Karma!*

*Use empty egg cartons as a packing material.* Containers made of foam or cardboard are great packing material alternatives. Foam egg cartons can also be used as an emergency ice cube tray, for example, or to organize small items in a desk or junk drawer.

*What you did...*

**You faked static, then hung up on your mother when she started talking about her plantar warts.**

## *Reverse Your Bad Karma!*

*Drive an elderly neighbor to a doctor's appointment.* Getting to and from appointments may seem mundane to healthy, young, energetic individuals, but it can be a major headache for an elderly person without easy and accessible transportation.

*What you did . . .*

**You wrote messages on your friend's back in sunscreen when he asked you to rub it in. Now he has the words "I'm Stupid!" in white, and a sunburn everywhere else.**

## *Reverse Your Bad Karma!*

*Do your part to clean our shores.* Join the worldwide effort to clean up trash lying along the shorelines of the world's oceans, rivers, and lakes.

*What you did . . .*

**Your grandma is convinced that her aide is stealing her forks . . . but it's really you.**

## *Reverse Your Bad Karma!*

*Repair an elderly neighbor's house.* Find a way to put carpenters and others together with organizations that can help with funding. Repair the house or raise up a new one so that the elderly occupant is safe again.

*What you did ...*

**You let your teenager's metal band, The Ear Exploders, practice in your apartment at 6 A.M. every Saturday.**

## *Reverse Your Bad Karma!*

*Give your old musical instrument to a school music program.* There are many school-age children throughout America who do not have the financial means to purchase a musical instrument.

*What you did . . .*

**You blamed your assistant for a mistake you made.**

## *Reverse Your Bad Karma!*

*Participate in career day at your local high school.* Volunteer to talk about your career and inspire young teens to enter your field of work.

*What you did...*

**After your spouse went to sleep, you stayed up to check her text messages.**

## *Reverse Your Bad Karma!*

*Show an interest in your loved one's work or career.* When you were growing up you may have had no idea where your parents went every day, but there's no excuse for not taking an interest as an adult.

*What you did . . .*

**You lied on your resume about volunteering at a nursing home. (No one will suspect, even if the residents don't remember you!)**

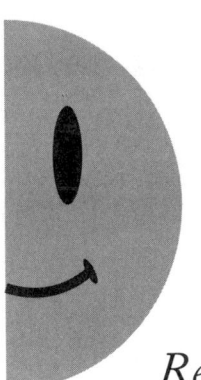

## *Reverse Your Bad Karma!*

*Volunteer at a local hospital.* Variously called Candy Stripers and Pink Ladies, volunteers (men are included, too) serve an important function in hospitals that are often understaffed. Volunteers can rock babies to sleep, operate the hospitality cart offering magazines and gum, fetch wheelchairs, and transport discharged patients to their cars.

*What you did . . .*

**You trained your dog to defend your home from intruders . . . by using your mother-in-law's blouse.**

## *Reverse Your Bad Karma!*

*Set a good example for your children.* Be respectful toward others and exhibit good manners. When you say "yes, ma'am," and "yes, sir," you are showing respect. Don't forget to say "please" and "thank you." In a bygone era, young people used to learn proper etiquette and manners in finishing schools. Now it is up to parents to teach youngsters how to conduct themselves in social situations.

*What you did...*

**You packed mustard and a raw egg for your child's lunch.**

## *Reverse Your Bad Karma!*

*Teach a child to cook.* Make sure the project is age appropriate and the child's safety is ensured. Make it fun and easy. Cooking together will instill confidence in the child and provide a way for you to spend quality time together.

*What you did...*

**You poured bleach into your roommate's shampoo bottle.**

## *Reverse Your Bad Karma!*

*Leave an encouraging message on the fridge.* A simple note in the morning can make someone happy all day long. Try, "Hey, your hair looks way more interesting that way!" on a sticky note.

*What you did . . .*

**You sold your son's comic book collection on eBay . . . and pocketed the cash for yourself.**

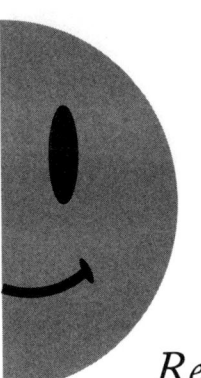

## *Reverse Your Bad Karma!*

*Stop being a constant consumer.* Vow to not be a part of the dramatically escalating consumption standard. We buy more things than we need and find that purchasing them does not yield long-term happiness. Instead of using our money in ways to give us a leisure society, we buy more, and then have to work harder to earn more.

*What you did ...*

**When you visited your newborn at the hospital, you pretended that the prettiest baby was yours—the one next to your child.**

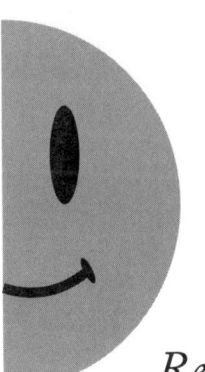

## *Reverse Your Bad Karma!*

*Make tiny hats for preemies.* Donate these knitted caps to your local hospital or a family you know who's recently had a premature baby. Make the hats from washed and dried soft cotton. Call the hospital neonatal unit to find out if they have rules or criteria for making such items.

*What you did . . .*

**You pretended to be interested in a charity to hit on the cute volunteer, but gave them fake credit card information for your monthly donation.**

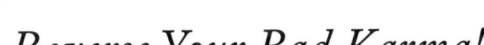

## *Reverse Your Bad Karma!*

*Hold a benefit.* People love gathering together for worthy causes, and it makes the act of donating more sociable. If you can't attend or organize one on your own, consider volunteering for a benefit. With people like you volunteering to serve food, the overhead costs are lowered, and more of the proceeds can go directly to the organization.

*What you did . . .*

**You had your child call your office with an "emergency" so that you could take the rest of the day off.**

## *Reverse Your Bad Karma!*

*Teach children to always tell the truth.* With the way modern media presents information, it is sometimes difficult to separate fact from fiction. With infomercials, infotainment, and edutainment bombarding us, we get many sides of a story, many topics skewed or "spun," but we don't always know what is true and what is not. Your child is in the same quandary. Show him or her what a truth teller looks like, sounds like, and is like.

*What you did . . .*
# You broke up a royal couple.

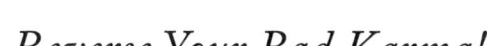

## *Reverse Your Bad Karma!*

*Play matchmaker.* Have a party and invite two people you know would hit it off. Introduce them at the party and see what happens. Who knows . . . they may spend the rest of their married life thanking you!

*What you did . . .*

**You dared someone to stare directly at the sun. You double-dog dared them.**

## *Reverse Your Bad Karma!*

*Go solar.* Consider making your house solar; you'll save money on electricity and do the earth a favor at the same time.

*What you did . . .*

**You sent yourself an elaborate gift basket from a "secret admirer" to keep your partner on his toes.**

## *Reverse Your Bad Karma!*

*Give the gift of organically grown flowers.* These naturally harvested bouquets will brighten someone's day and have a much smaller carbon footprint than hothouse flowers.

*What you did . . .*

**You snuck into a confession booth on a Sunday morning and posed as a priest to learn your neighbors' secrets.**

## *Reverse Your Bad Karma!*

*Do not judge others.* Try to understand them. It is much better to judge yourself and change what you do not like after a period of honest introspection.

*What you did . . .*

**You replaced your roommate's high heels with only left shoes.**

## Reverse Your Bad Karma!

*Teach a child how to tie her shoelaces.* If you see a child running around with her shoes untied, ask her if she wants you to help tie them. Demonstrate how to tie the laces with one shoe, and then let her practice on her other shoe.

*What you did . . .*

**You made a beer run for a bunch of teenagers.**

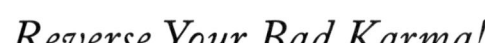

## *Reverse Your Bad Karma!*

*Become a Big Brother or Big Sister volunteer.* Your commitment could have a positive impact on the life of a young person. For example, more than half of the kids with a Big Brother or Big Sister are less inclined to ditch school, and roughly 46 percent steer clear of ever using illegal substances.

*What you did . . .*

**You went through your neighbor's mailbox and took their coupon sheets.**

## *Reverse Your Bad Karma!*

*Be a pen pal to someone in the military.* No one wants to feel alone and forgotten. This is a way to help a soldier serving in a foreign land know he has a friend.

*What you did . . .*

**You lied to your doctor about back pain in order to get a prescription for medical marijuana. He prescribed aspirin instead.**

## *Reverse Your Bad Karma!*

*Host a charity fundraiser for a health-related cause.* Whether it's an informal potluck hosted at your house, or a black tie event at a fancy restaurant, you can bring your friends, family members, coworkers, and neighbors together for a good cause. Collect donations at the door or charge per plate and then donate all the proceeds to a world health cause.

*What you did . . .*

**You ate all of your children's Halloween candy. You told them the Tooth Fairy did it.**

## *Reverse Your Bad Karma!*

*Help provide safe drinking water for children.* According to the World Health Organization, more than 3.4 million lives, mostly young children, are lost each year because of water-related diseases, the leading cause of death worldwide. Four thousand children die each day because of diseases related to the organisms thriving in the filthy drinking water they consume. Find and fund programs for safe drinking water.

*What you did . . .*

**You left an urgent and vague message on a coworker's voicemail, with a callback number to an Elvis sighting hotline.**

## *Reverse Your Bad Karma!*

*Invite the new hire out to lunch.* Starting a new job is hard. One of the reasons being you don't know the people with whom you work. Help the new person in your office out and invite him to lunch.

*What you did . . .*
**You pretended to be a Nigerian prince who needed a loan.**

## Reverse Your Bad Karma!

*Fight malaria.* This preventable and curable parasitic-born disease kills roughly a million people each year, 90 percent of them children in Africa. Malaria is caused by a parasite that is carried by mosquitoes that infect people. Many of the world's poorest, especially woman and children, are at highest risk and once infected have little or no resources to deal with the disease.

*What you did . . .*

**You ate an entire cheese pizza while watching the exercise video your doctor recommended.**

## *Reverse Your Bad Karma!*

*Plant an apple tree.* Not only does it benefit the environment, it will produce fruits that are low in calories and high in fiber.

*What you did* . . .

**You punched your daughter's soccer coach when he kept her on the bench.**

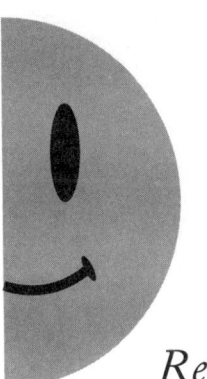

## *Reverse Your Bad Karma!*

*Encourage your children to be considerate.* They should know how to act when in public places like houses of worship, restaurants, and stores. Unruly children can ruin an enjoyable experience for someone else if they are being disruptive.

*What you did...*

**You buried your neighbor's car in snow until only the antenna was showing.**

## *Reverse Your Bad Karma!*

*Mow a neighbor's yard.* If you have promised in the past to mow another person's yard and forgot, write yourself a note and make a point to follow through on your promise. Do the honorable thing.

*What you did . . .*
**You found a valuable ring on the sidewalk. You're using it as a Monopoly piece.**

## *Reverse Your Bad Karma!*

*Shovel the snow from your neighbor's steps.* Shoveling snow can be a very arduous task. Help out your neighbors who might need an extra hand. Offer to shovel their steps, driveway, and walkway, and only take their "thank you" as compensation.

*What you did* . . .

**You gave your best friend's boyfriend mono—the kissing disease. Now all three of you have it.**

## *Reverse Your Bad Karma!*

*Be a hug millionaire.* Generously give hugs to children, senior citizens, coworkers, teachers, friends, parents, siblings, and your pet. This small act of affection will brighten everyone's day.

*What you did . . .*

**You broke your friend's 3D glasses halfway through the movie.**

## *Reverse Your Bad Karma!*

*Donate used prescription eyeglasses and frames.* Check with your local eye doctor about community organizations that collect old eyeglasses and frames, and donate them to those who cannot afford them.

*What you did . . .*

**You spread rumors around the school that you're a vampire, and now the *Twilight* fans do all of your homework for you.**

## *Reverse Your Bad Karma!*

*Donate blood.* It's quick, fairly painless, and you could be saving a life.

*What you did . . .*

**You took a 70 percent cut of your child's lemonade stand profits. (Hey, those paper cups didn't buy themselves!)**

## *Reverse Your Bad Karma!*

*Attend a local school's fundraiser.* These events raise money for a particular student group. Whether the school is sponsoring a performance of a well-known play to raise money for the theatrical department or hosting a spaghetti dinner to raise money for the band, enjoy an evening at your local school and help the students reach their financial goals.

*What you did . . .*
# You executed the perfect Ponzi scheme.

## Reverse Your Bad Karma!

*Show good manners.* Respect, tact, diplomacy, and hospitality are all reflected in good manners. Don't interrupt, greet elderly people and women first, don't shout, return greetings and goodbyes, keep your elbows off the table, and chew with your mouth closed. Sloppy manners suggest a careless disregard for others. Conversely, good manners suggest good upbringing and consideration of others.

*What you did . . .*

**You pushed an annoying commuter out of the subway car right before the doors closed. (Who plays Angry Birds with the sound on, anyway?)**

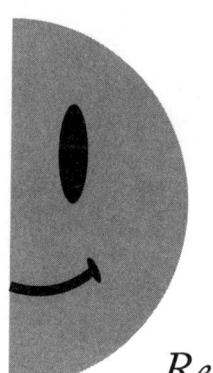

## *Reverse Your Bad Karma!*

*Learn how to give positive criticism and feedback.* Giving and receiving criticism is not easy. Finding fault is easy, but finding fault isn't the point. Offer honest criticism in private. Be calm and thoughtful when making your point. Show a spirit of concern and a desire to help. If it's a project that is the focus of the criticism, explain what isn't working and why. Focus on the problem, not the person. Offer suggestions for fixing the problem or making the project better. Solicit feedback to make sure the other person understands the point you are making.

# REVERSE YOUR BAD KARMA
## FOR NATURE

# "It's going to take at least three of us to tip that cow."

—Joe Schmoe

"Never doubt that a small group of thoughtful, committed citizens can change the world."

—Margaret Mead

*What you did...*

**You killed ants with a magnifying glass.**

## *Reverse Your Bad Karma!*

*Protect endangered species of birds.* Do something to help ensure that the Whooping Crane, the Mexican Spotted Owl, the Ivory-billed Woodpecker, and the Puerto Rican Parrot, along with hundreds of other birds on the endangered species watch list, do not go extinct.

*What you did . . .*

**You bought pants made out of seal skin—baby seal skin.**

## *Reverse Your Bad Karma!*

*Give coats and jackets to relief organizations.* Go through your closets and find the ones you no longer wear. Put them in a box and donate them to help people in cold climates survive the cold weather.

*What you did . . .*

**While your boss was on vacation you watered his office plant . . . with diet soda.**

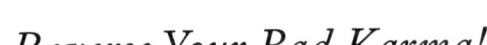

## *Reverse Your Bad Karma!*

*Be frugal with water while brushing your teeth.* Rinse to get the brush wet and rinse to clean the brush when you have finished brushing. Don't leave the water running the whole time. Use only what you need. You'll soon discover that you don't really need much water to brush.

*What you did ...*

**You told a child that cats will fly if you pull hard enough on their tails.**

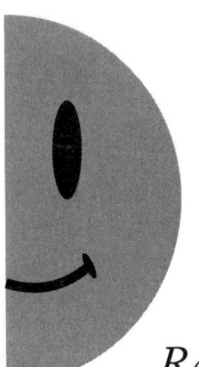

## *Reverse Your Bad Karma!*

*Watch a pet while its owner is on vacation.* Whether the pet is an iguana or a horse, take the responsibility seriously and care for the animal exactly as you are instructed. Make certain you have phone numbers and know how to deal with any emergencies that may arise.

*What you did . . .*

**You forgot to turn off your air conditioner before going on a two-week vacation.**

## *Reverse Your Bad Karma!*

*Plant a tree.* Urban forests help improve air quality. Trees absorb carbon dioxide and release oxygen into the atmosphere. One tree gives enough oxygen back through photosynthesis to support two human beings.

*What you did...*

**You fed your parakeet its own eggs, sunny-side up.**

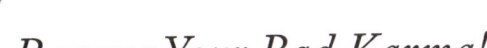

## *Reverse Your Bad Karma!*

*Buy fresh eggs from a local farm.* This will help both the farm and you. Your purchase will help with the daily maintenance and possible expansion of the farm. And the fresh eggs will taste better in your omelets, salads, and cakes.

*What you did . . .*

**You tried to smuggle an exotic animal through airport security.**

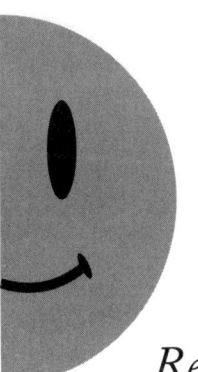

## *Reverse Your Bad Karma!*

*Carry a piece of luggage for a stranger.* Help an elderly person or mom with a stroller carry large pieces of luggage. Chances are they have been toting those big bags around for a while now and could use the help.

*What you did . . .*

**You served a vegetarian mock chicken . . . made of beef.**

## *Reverse Your Bad Karma!*

*Avoid eating meat when dining with a vegetarian.* Show your friend some respect. She may not mind that you are eating a nonvegetarian meal, but if you haven't already cleared it with her, just try abstaining from meat for one evening. It won't hurt you, and it could actually be good for you.

*What you did* . . .

**You stole a monkey from the zoo so that you could buy him an accordion and make money by panhandling.**

## *Reverse Your Bad Karma!*

*Establish a wildlife refuge in your garden.* All you need to do is supply three things: a protected area where birds can nest, food (living plants as well as seeds, nuts, berries, suet, etc., that you supply), and clean water (bird bath, fountain, etc.). Watch as your little sanctuary fills with life and thrives.

*What you did...*

**You gave your dog gum and tried to teach it to blow bubbles.**

## *Reverse Your Bad Karma!*

*Raise awareness about spaying and neutering.* Spaying and neutering animals reduces the growing populations of stray dogs and cats and can have an added benefit of reducing the incidents of humans being bitten by such animals infected with rabies or other diseases.

*What you did...*

**You chopped down a tree just to count the rings and find out how old it was. (One hundred and twenty-three years.)**

## *Reverse Your Bad Karma!*

*Save America's parks.* Many are in crisis with deteriorating roads, trails, and visitors' facilities. Some parks are operating without adequate funding. Pollution and traffic congestion exacts a toll on these national treasures.

*What you did . . .*
**You salted a slug.**

## *Reverse Your Bad Karma!*

*Cut the plastic rings of any six-pack beverage carrier. Those plastic holders can make it into the ocean where they are harmful to dolphins and other sea life.*

*What you did . . .*

**You put a turtle on its back to watch it try to get up.**

## *Reverse Your Bad Karma!*

*Help a wounded animal.* Stop and call for aid if you see an animal wounded in a vehicle accident. Contact a local wildlife shelter or emergency veterinarian clinic.

*What you did . . .*

**You ate a member of an endangered species. (We hear that Bengal Tiger is excellent grilled with a lemon herb marinade.)**

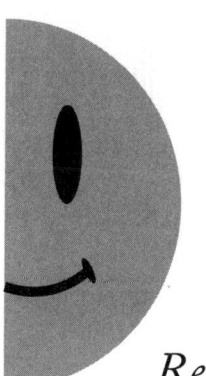

## *Reverse Your Bad Karma!*

*Sponsor an acre of rain forest.* Make a $40 donation in someone's name—like the tiger's.

*What you did...*

**You let a skunk loose in a rival team's locker room.**

## *Reverse Your Bad Karma!*

*Rescue a stuck cat.* If you notice a cat trapped up a tree or telephone pole and can get to it without risking your own safety, help it down. Otherwise, call the fire department, local humane society, or other animal rescue organization. If they can't do the rescue, they can help you find someone who can.

*What you did...*

**You threw a candy bar wrapper out of your car window while you were driving on the highway. (Hey, it's either that or litter inside your sweet ride, right?)**

## *Reverse Your Bad Karma!*

*Use a lunchbox.* Instead of a using a paper bag each day to carry your sandwich and drink, opt for this reusable alternative. This is a great way to reduce paper waste.

*What you did . . .*

**You're growing pot in your parents' basement.**

## *Reverse Your Bad Karma!*

*Freshen a friend's garden with herbs.* Grow some potted herbs such as lavender, mint, and basil. When a friend is going through a rough time or just feeling a little blue, take her this refreshing new addition to her garden.

*What you did . . .*
# You had a Styrofoam bonfire in your local reservation.

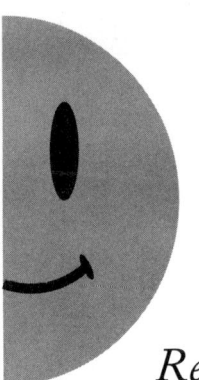

## Reverse Your Bad Karma!

*Stop using pesticides.* These chemical treatments can harm the planet and run off into water supplies. Find organic solutions to deter crop infestation, such as companion planting. Use damp newspapers placed on the ground at night in the garden to attract slugs. Then, the next morning, throw away the papers.

*What you did . . .*
## You peed in the ocean.

## *Reverse Your Bad Karma!*

*Water your vacationing friend's lawn.* During a hot spell, turn on his sprinkler or bring yours over to his lawn. A thoughtful act like this will save your neighbor the effort and money it takes to replant a burnt lawn.

*What you did . . .*
# You bet on a cock-fighting tournament.

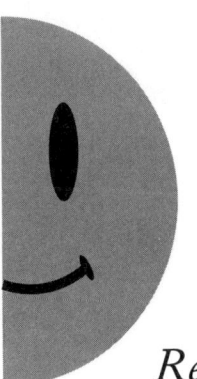

## *Reverse Your Bad Karma!*

*Rescue an injured bird.* Sometimes birds fall from their nests or smash into glass windows. In both cases, retrieve the bird (avoid overhandling) and place it in a dry box until the bird recovers, then return it to the wild.

*What you did . . .*

**The toasted marshmallow you tossed aside started a forest fire.**

## *Reverse Your Bad Karma!*

*Be a volunteer firefighter.* Help support the first line of defense that protects your community in the case of a fire. Pledge your time, hard work, and willpower to your local volunteer firefighting force.

*What you did...*

**You leave your refrigerator open at night so that you don't have to stumble for the light switch when you get up for your midnight snack.**

## *Reverse Your Bad Karma!*

*Keep your grocery shopping green.* Buy fresh foods and eggs in cardboard containers—avoid Styrofoam. When Americans buy food, roughly one dollar of every eleven spent goes for packaging and much of it ends up in landfills. Buy fresh produce. Purchase fresh meat wrapped in paper. Put items in a cloth bag for transporting them home.

*What you did* . . .
# You only eat *foie gras*, veal, and meat from caged chickens.

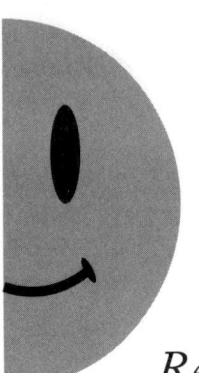

## *Reverse Your Bad Karma!*

*Promote healthy living.* Make sure your family is not only eating and exercising well, but is in a good state of mental health. Talk to them. Cheer them up. Get them to discuss their feelings. This is especially important for pregnant women, for in caring for their bodies and minds, they are directly affecting their unborn child.

*What you did...*

**You left your hose on during a drought. And you don't even have grass to water.**

## *Reverse Your Bad Karma!*

*Start a community garden.* Get members of your neighborhood and community to come together for this beautifying and eco-friendly endeavor. It creates green space in cities and gives gardeners a way to share the land, their skills, and their bounty with their community.

*What you did . . .*

**You threw a soda can in the trash, because it was an easier shot to make than the recycling bin. (Your imaginary fans would have been bummed if you'd missed, right?)**

## *Reverse Your Bad Karma!*

*Use both sides of the paper.* Print on one side of the paper, but if reprinting is necessary, do not throw that page away. Use the unprinted side of the paper for drafts of documents such as letters or manuscripts that will be used for making editing changes. Or use the other side for children's drawings that you can beautify your home with. When both sides are used, recycle the paper in your city or county's recycling bins or at a recycling center.

*What you did . . .*
# You named your horse "Glue Factory."

## *Reverse Your Bad Karma!*

*Be a foster caregiver to an abandoned animal.* If you cannot adopt but you could provide interim shelter, food, and veterinarian care for a helpless animal, consider being a foster care provider.

# REVERSE YOUR BAD KARMA FOR ORDER

# "I'm gonna chug five Bud Lights and go puke on that bum."

—Joe Schmoe

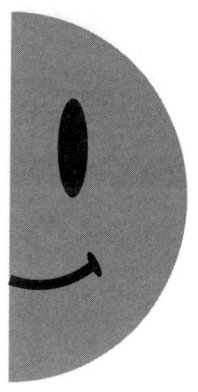

"You must be the change you wish to see in the world."

—Mahatma Gandhi

*What you did . . .*
# You cut in line at the DMV.

## *Reverse Your Bad Karma!*

*Put extra change in an expired parking meter.* As you're walking through your city center, check and see if anyone is parked at an expired meter. Pop a few coins in. If you have ever received a parking ticket, you probably wished that someone had done that for you.

*What you did . . .*

**You took one sock from every unattended dryer at the Laundromat.**

## *Reverse Your Bad Karma!*

*Recycle packing peanuts.* If you receive a package containing the small peanut-shaped foam bits that are commonly used as packing material, reuse them for another shipping.

*What you did . . .*

**You started a food fight in a middle school cafeteria . . . and you're the lunch lady.**

## *Reverse Your Bad Karma!*

*Take a class and learn about conflict resolution.* Apply it to the relationships in your life and watch how the causes of conflicts begin to shift or diminish.

*What you did...*

**You rewrote a Wikipedia article with the wrong information to avoid losing an argument. ("See, I *told* you that Paul McCartney wrote 'U Can't Touch This.'")**

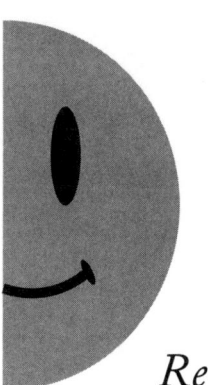

## *Reverse Your Bad Karma!*

*Go back to school.* If you have longed to return to school after the kids were grown, go for it. Make it your personal goal to get that degree or advanced degree. It's never too late to do something good for yourself, for your happiness at achieving your goal will affect everyone else around you.

*What you did . . .*

**You moved all of the cookies in the supermarket to the gluten-free shelf.**

## *Reverse Your Bad Karma!*

*Eat less meat.* On average, it costs much more to raise a herd of animals (feed, supplements, land, shelter, veterinarian costs, etc.) than to raise a field of beans or corn or produce other nonanimal sources of protein. The Federal Food and Drug Administration states that to eat for a healthy heart, you must cut down consumption of trans fats and saturated fats, most often found in food from animals. Eating less meat is a good thing to do for your body and the planet.

*What you did . . .*

**You shouted out the movie's twist ending during the trailers. (Bruce Willis was dead the whole time! Rosebud was the sled!)**

## *Reverse Your Bad Karma!*

*Open your mind through reading.* Start subscriptions to magazines not on your usual reading list. Read them with the intent of broadening your scope of knowledge about new subjects.

*What you did . . .*

**You left a note after you hit a parked car. That note was, "People saw me hit your car, so I'm pretending to leave you my insurance information. Good luck with that dent!"**

## *Reverse Your Bad Karma!*

*Drive a hybrid.* Cut down on the nasty emissions your gas-powered automobile releases by opting for a hybrid the next time you buy or lease a car. Not only will opting for a hybrid help save the earth, it will also save you some money at the gas pump.

*What you did . . .*

**You took all the change from the "Take a Penny, Leave a Penny" jar. You didn't leave a penny.**

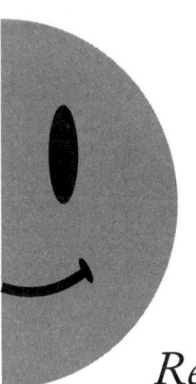

## *Reverse Your Bad Karma!*

*Pick up trash.* If you see litter, don't just let it bother you; get out there and pick it up!

*What you did . . .*

**You stole a priceless piece of art . . . and used it as a coaster.**

## *Reverse Your Bad Karma!*

*Adopt a section of a highway.* Keep it clean and picturesque. Organize a group to help pick up trash along your designated section of the road. It goes a long way toward keeping America beautiful.

*What you did . . .*

**When you saw someone running to catch your elevator before the doors closed, you moved forward to hold it open, but didn't get there in time—on purpose.**

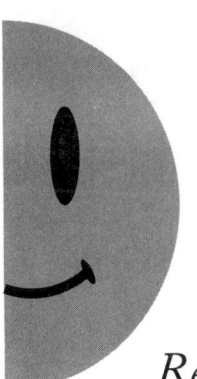

## *Reverse Your Bad Karma!*

*Give up your seat on a bus.* Whether it's to an elderly person, a pregnant woman, a young mother with several children, a physically challenged person, or simply someone who looks weary, giving your seat up will help that person out and brighten his or her day.

*What you did . . .*
**You jaywalked.**

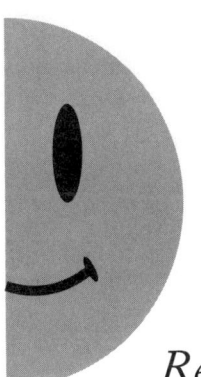

## *Reverse Your Bad Karma!*

*Support the local police.* Make a contribution to the police officers' association charitable foundation in your city. The money usually supports widow and orphan groups, college scholarships, youth leagues, drug resistance programs, victim support, and senior programs, among other worthwhile activities.

*What you did . . .*

**You ordered "one of everything" from a fast-food drive-thru, while a line of cars stretched behind you.**

## *Reverse Your Bad Karma!*

*Over-tip a good waiter or waitress.* Remember, much of what they make is dependent on the generosity of people like you.

*What you did . . .*

**You hired a professor to write your child's college admissions essay.**

## *Reverse Your Bad Karma!*

*Donate bookcases to a school library.* If you have an old bookcase that's just collecting dust, contact your local school and see if they can put it to good use. Most schools are always looking for small pieces of furniture like bookcases.

*What you did . . .*
## You didn't say, "Bless you," when someone sneezed.

## *Reverse Your Bad Karma!*

*Take a meal to a sick neighbor.* No one wants to cook when they are sick. Your gesture will mean a lot to the person who is ill.

*What you did . . .*
## You cheated at Scrabble.

## *Reverse Your Bad Karma!*

*Play chess with an older relative.* See if a grandparent, or great aunt or uncle wants to play a game of chess. Take your set to the park and enjoy the sounds of nature. The game and surroundings will be therapeutic for you both.

*What you did . . .*

**You and your friends always walk *slooooowly* down the sidewalk, shoulder-to-shoulder, so that nobody can get around you.**

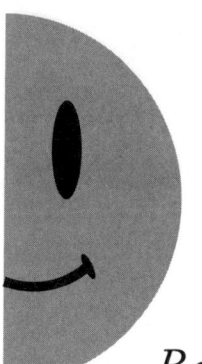

## *Reverse Your Bad Karma!*

*Help a young family off the plane.* Parents traveling with small children have plenty to carry—babies, diaper bags, toys, and a stroller. They were allowed to board first, but the same is not true for when the plane lands and they have to disembark. If you are seated near them, do what you can to help them get off.

*What you did . . .*

**You brought thirty items into the "Ten or Less" express checkout line at the grocery store. When someone called you on it, you pretended not to speak English.**

## *Reverse Your Bad Karma!*

*Ride your bike to the grocery store.* If you're going to pick up a small amount of items, don't take the car. It's better for the environment to keep cars off the road whenever possible.

*What you did . . .*

**You're stealing cable from the apartment next to yours.**

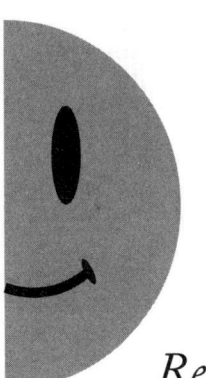

## *Reverse Your Bad Karma!*

*Unplug electrical items not in use.* Some cell phone chargers, for example, continue to use electrical current even after a cell phone has been removed from it.

*What you did...*

**You faked whiplash for an insurance settlement after a fender bender.**

## *Reverse Your Bad Karma!*

*Remind friends to get their checkups.* Screenings can detect early breast cancer, colon cancer, prostate problems, heart disease, and a number of other potentially life-threatening illnesses. Many people put off getting health checkups. Don't let them.

*What you did . . .*
# You tore the tag off of your mattress.

## *Reverse Your Bad Karma!*

*Say "no thanks" to fresh linens daily.* Some hotels have a system where only towels left on the floor will be replaced with new ones. Think about how often you wash your towels at home and decide if you really need fresh ones daily; you'll be doing the environment a favor by reusing.

*What you did . . .*

**You took a cab . . . while running the New York City Marathon.**

## *Reverse Your Bad Karma!*

*Coach a children's sports team.* If you don't know how to play the particular sport, volunteer to help the coach and do whatever is needed. Demonstrate good sportsmanship on the ball field, ice rink, or gymnastics floor.

*What you did . . .*

**To impress a crush, you pretended to have understood James Joyce's *Ulysses*. You haven't even read it.**

## *Reverse Your Bad Karma!*

*Donate old books to schools.* Look at your bookshelf and ask yourself if you're really ever going to reread each one. Schools can put used books to good use either through their loan system or by selling them at a used book sale and putting the profits toward buying new books.

*What you did* . . .
# You wrapped a car with plastic wrap.

## *Reverse Your Bad Karma!*

*Support your local high school's car wash.* Get your car washed by high school students during their car wash fundraiser. While it might not get your car as clean as a professional wash, your contribution will make a difference and help the community's schools.

*What you did . . .*
# You caused the collapse of the Euro.

## *Reverse Your Bad Karma!*

*Buy a homeless person a hot meal.* It doesn't have to be an expensive sit-down dinner. A hungry person needs nutrition and nourishment of the body and soul. The face of homelessness in America includes families with children. Poverty is frightening for many of us because deep down we may fear a reversal of fortune in our own lives.

*What you did . . .*

**You borrowed the kids in the neighborhood for the picture you'll use on your yearly Christmas cards—when you'll pretend that you're an incredibly successful tycoon with a sprawling multicultural family.**

## Reverse Your Bad Karma!

*Babysit for a single parent or family in need for free.* Childcare costs can be a huge burden and can often stop a single parent from earning their much-needed maximum potential income. If you can offer to help for a couple of hours here and there you'll be doing a great service.

*What you did . . .*

**You didn't replace the toilet paper when you finished the roll.**

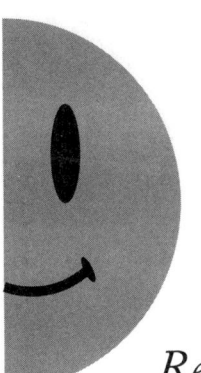

## *Reverse Your Bad Karma!*

*Refill the copier's paper tray.* The next time you use your office copier, put more paper in the paper tray. This simple act will save someone else time when she goes to make copies.

*What you did . . .*

**You spilled red wine on a white carpet, then blamed it on an "earthquake" that no one else noticed.**

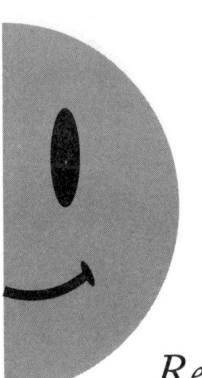

## *Reverse Your Bad Karma!*

*Notify neighbors about severe weather warnings.* Forewarned is forearmed. If they are elderly or physically disabled, offer to help them secure their home.

*What you did . . .*
**You ran a red light.**

## *Reverse Your Bad Karma!*

*Help someone cross a busy street.* Be it a woman navigating a stroller with other children in tow, an elderly person with a bag of groceries, a man with a white cane, a child on a bike, a homeless veteran with a shopping cart, or anyone else who looks like he or she could use a little help—offer them some help.

*What you did . . .*

**You took all of the sugar packets from your local coffee shop.**

## *Reverse Your Bad Karma!*

*Drink fair trade coffee.* As more people become aware of the importance of fair trade products, it's getting easier to make smart choices, so why not start with the coffee you drink every morning? Make sure to check the label when you're buying coffee for the "fair trade certified" logo. Even large chains like Starbucks are now selling fair trade coffee, so there's no excuse not to make this smart choice.

*What you did . . .*
# You took up two spaces in a mall parking lot on Black Friday.

## *Reverse Your Bad Karma!*

*Help unload a neighbor's car.* If you see a neighbor unloading his or her bags from the car after a shopping trip, offer to help take them inside.

*What you did . . .*

**You keyed a car that took up two spaces in a mall parking lot on Black Friday.**

## *Reverse Your Bad Karma!*

*Resist road rage.* Instead of giving inconsiderate drivers the finger, slamming on your horn, yelling at your kids, or chewing out an employee when you get to work, count to ten and breathe deeply. Redirect the urge to lash out by counting and breathing deeply.

*What you did . . .*

**You taught a foreign exchange student the wrong words on purpose. (A "hamster" is what you use to write on paper! "Waffle" means slightly wet!)**

## *Reverse Your Bad Karma!*

*Clean up your language.* It's easy to fall into the habit of using bad English, slang, and profanity. Make an effort to speak better English. Excellent language skills improve your personal image wherever you go in the world, and you will be setting a good example for others.

*What you did . . .*

**You called in sick to work to get a head start on your beach weekend.**

## *Reverse Your Bad Karma!*

*Write a thank-you note to a coworker.* The next time he helps you with a project or a problem, take a minute to show your appreciation. A simple thank-you might do, but a note shows your appreciation at a whole new level.

*What you did . . .*

**You impersonated a policeman to get free coffee and donuts.**

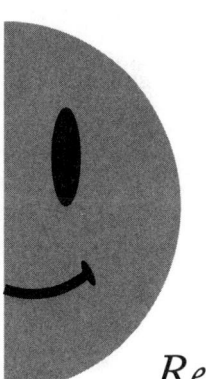

## *Reverse Your Bad Karma!*

*Adopt a bench at a local park.* Use a plaque to memorialize a role model or someone special who has passed on. Attach the plaque to the bench's back support.

*What you did . . .*

**You hit all of the floor numbers in the elevator while everyone else was trying to head home on a Friday afternoon.**

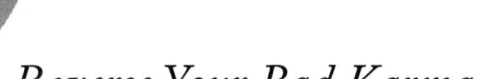

## *Reverse Your Bad Karma!*

*Open a door for someone carrying packages.* Lend an extra hand to someone who needs it. If you see someone juggling a bunch of packages, go grab the door for them. This little extra effort will help prevent any tumbling and breaking.

*What you did . . .*

**In homage to your favorite early 1990s hip hop song, you spray painted "Hammer Time!" on all of your town's stop signs.**

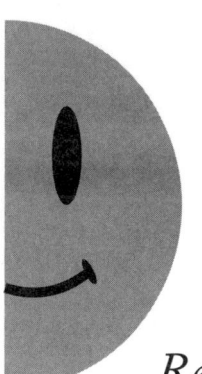

## *Reverse Your Bad Karma!*

*Brighten up a wall with a mural.* Find an open spot in your neighborhood or a local park and invite local schoolchildren to help you. Your mural could make a statement of cultural pride or feature images of people working together. Your city or town may even pay for the supplies.

*What you did . . .*

**You incited a riot at your anger management group's therapy session.**

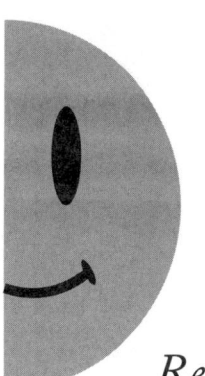

## *Reverse Your Bad Karma!*

*Practice patience and serenity.* The next time you start to feel agitated, try counting to ten or following your breath in and out. Such practices help to provide a counter-balance to the effects of daily stress.

*What you did* . . .
# You broke into someone's house and rearranged their furniture.

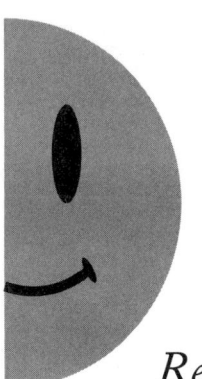

## *Reverse Your Bad Karma!*

*House-sit for a friend while she goes on vacation.* She will have peace of mind about her home (and possibly pets, if you are watching them as well) and can focus on her much-needed vacation.

*What you did . . .*
# You took all the free samples.

## Reverse Your Bad Karma!

*Help someone out at the grocery store.* Reach high to retrieve a grocery item for someone who wants it but can't reach it. If neither of you can reach it, offer to summon help.

*What you did . . .*

**You broke a figurine in a boutique and hid it behind another item. Then you quickly left, brushing past the "You Break It, You Buy It" sign.**

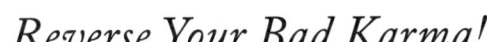

## *Reverse Your Bad Karma!*

*Donate the profits of resold garage sale finds.* Go to garage sales and pick up items in good condition. Clean them well and put them for sale on eBay. Donate the money you make to your favorite charity.

*What you did . . .*

**You've been switching around the political yard signs in your neighborhood.**

## *Reverse Your Bad Karma!*

*Get involved in community politics.* Involvement is the only way to get your voice heard. Attend town meetings and help solve local homelessness, panhandling, and other problems that involve the entire community.

*What you did . . .*

**You switched the labels for the regular and decaf coffee at an evening PTA meeting.**

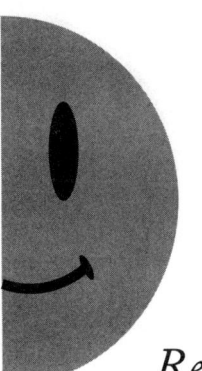

## *Reverse Your Bad Karma!*

*Recycle your coffee grounds.* Keep an empty coffee can handy in your kitchen to collect the grounds after brewing. You can either deposit them in your compost or use them as fertilizer in your garden.

*What you did* . . .
# You dog-eared a library book.

## *Reverse Your Bad Karma!*

*Read to the blind.* You can help record audio versions of newspapers, books, and magazines for the visually impaired.

*What you did . . .*

**You never remove the lint from the dryer.**

## *Reverse Your Bad Karma!*

*Do a friend's dishes.* Clear and do the dishes the next time you have dinner at a friend, neighbor, or acquaintance's house. It shows good manners and is a great way to thank her for having you over.

*What you did . . .*

**You are pretending to be the secret, illegitimate love-child of a rock star and a Hollywood starlet to get preferred VIP treatment at a hotel.**

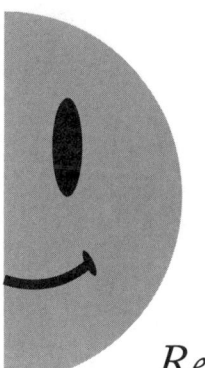

## *Reverse Your Bad Karma!*

*Be courteous to those serving you.* Remember to tip the domestics, waiters, captain, sommelier, rest room attendant, doorman, and limousine driver. Say please and thank you, no matter who you're pretending to be.

*What you did* . . .
# You faked a seizure to get out of taking a test.

## *Reverse Your Bad Karma!*

*Learn to perform the Heimlich maneuver.* Use it if you see someone choking or unable to cough up food or a foreign object. This simple procedure is easy to learn and could save a life. Teach it to your family and friends.

*What you did . . .*

**You've been sneaking into your office's refrigerator and eating the best parts of everyone's lunch.**

## *Reverse Your Bad Karma!*

*Bring in a box of donuts for everyone.* Sharing a sweet treat will improve camaraderie among your coworkers.

*What you did . . .*

**You prank called your state senator. (Is your refrigerator running? You better watch out, I might vote for that instead!)**

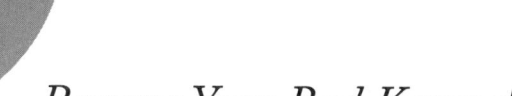

## *Reverse Your Bad Karma!*

*Make your vote count.* Research the politicians that you're voting for and familiarize yourself with their positions on war. Make sure that it is in line with your own feelings before casting your vote.

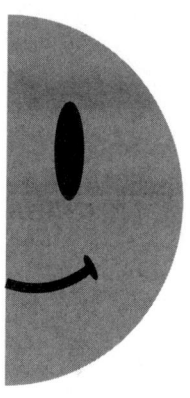

# Reverse Your Book!

Pssst! Have you canceled out all of your bad deeds? Good job, you have a clean karma slate!

But maybe it's just a little too clean? Now that you're doing nothing but good deeds, you run the risk of sending your karma too far the other way. Balance is key. And no one likes a goody two-shoes.

It's time to Reverse Your Book!

Make a list of all of the wonderful things you've done. Now go through the book again, but start on the right-hand page this time. Did you drink fair trade coffee this morning? Good job! Feel free to steal some sugar packets this afternoon.

Don't worry about going overboard. If you ever get too close to the dark side, just flip to the beginning of the book and start again!

# Acknowledgments

I'd like to thank Halli, Ross, Victoria, Kate, Brendan, Meredith, and the rest of the team at Adams Media. You're all sociopaths with hearts of gold.

**"I'm just going to help myself to those cigarettes behind the counter. Put that on my tab."**

—Joe Schmoe

"No man can sincerely try to help another without helping himself."

—Ralph Waldo Emerson